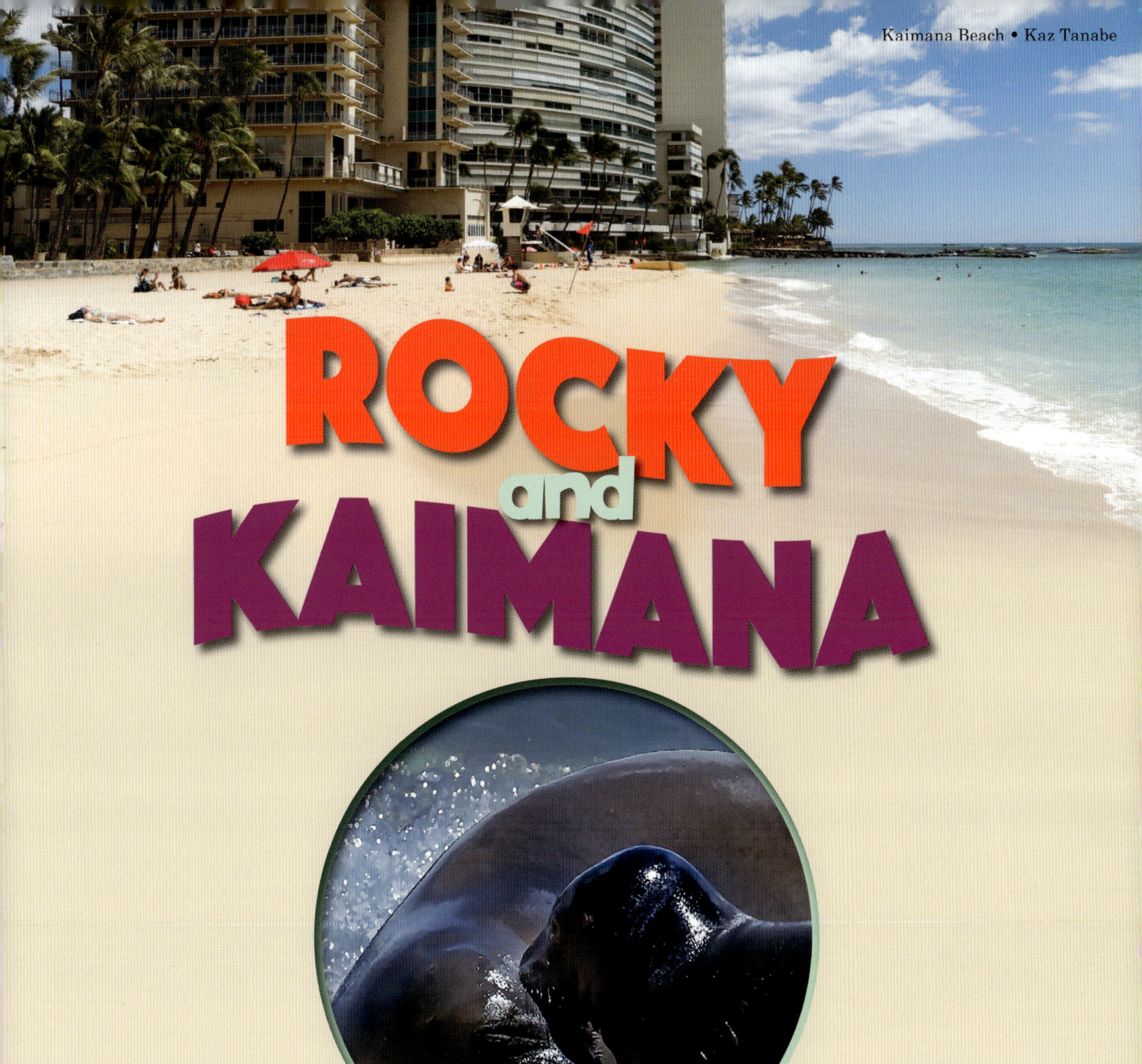

Kaimana Beach • Kaz Tanabe

ROCKY
and
KAIMANA

Melody Bentz Photography

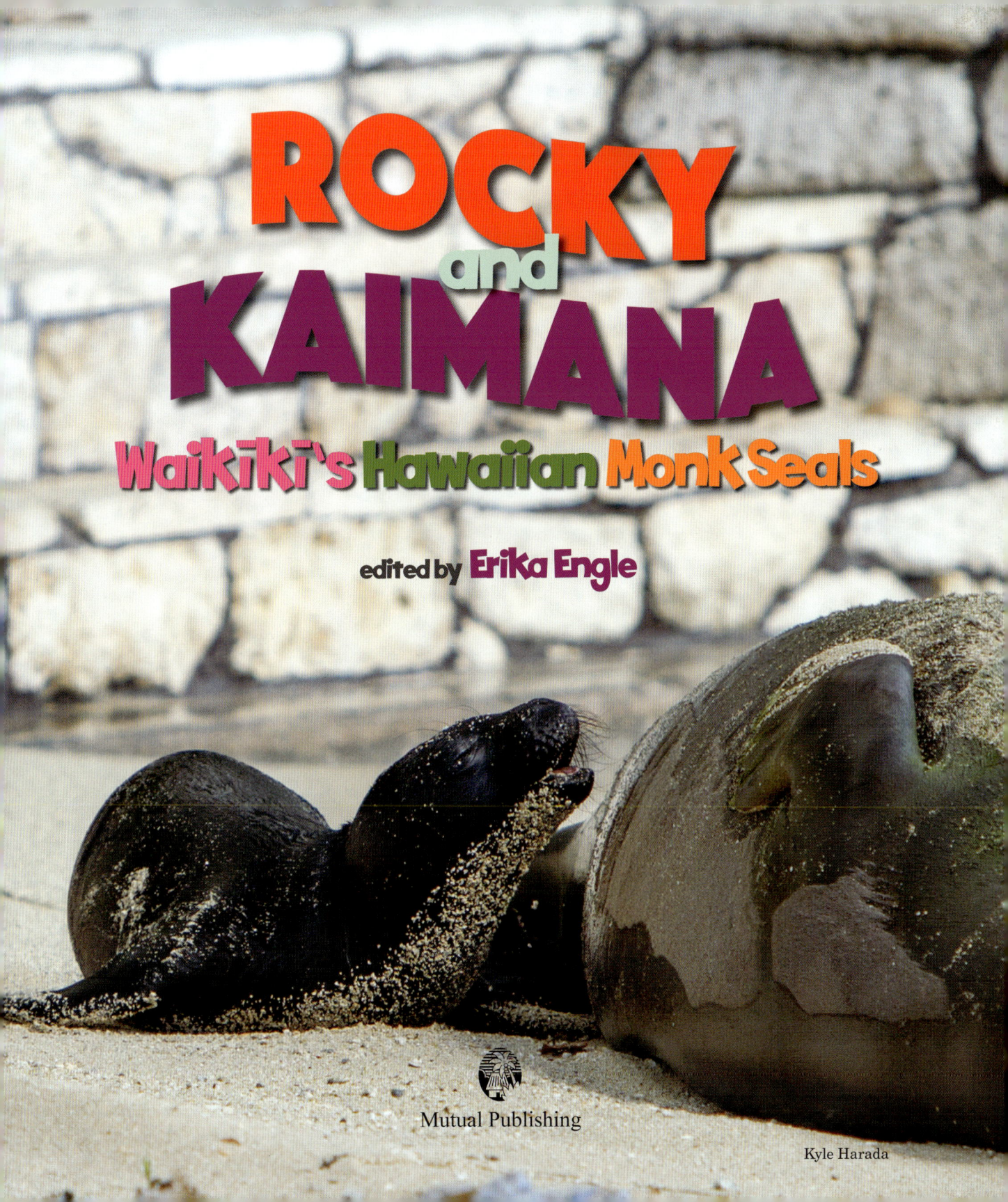

ROCKY and KAIMANA
Waikīkī's Hawaiian Monk Seals

edited by **Erika Engle**

Mutual Publishing

Kyle Harada

Melody Bentz Photography

Photos © *Honolulu Star-Advertiser:*
  Bruce Asato pg. 20, 28 (top), 29 (bottom), 32, 33
  Jim Borg pg. 34, 35
  Craig T. Kojima pg. 21, 28 (bottom), 29 (top), 31, 40
  Dennis Oda pg. 10 (bottom), 24, 26 (top), 27, 38-39, 44 (right)
  Cindy Ellen Russell pg. 2 (both inset), 11, 12, 14, 15, 16 (left),
    17, 18, 19, 26 (sign), 30, 41, 44 (left)

Photos © Melody Bentz Photography: front cover (bottom),
  backcover (inset), pg. 1 (inset), 4, 5, 8-9, 23 (bottom), 36, 37, 48
Photo © DB Dunlap: pg. 6-7
Photo © Marilyn Dunlap: pg. 22 (top)
Photos © Kyle Harada: pg. 3, 16 (right)
Photo © Gayle Matsuda: pg. 22 (inset), 23 (top)

Photos © Douglas Peebles: pg 2 (background), 10 (both inset),
  24-25, 43
Photos © Kaz Tanabe: front and back cover (top), pg. 1 (top), 42
Photos © Waikiki Aquarium: pg. 45

Spot illustrations from Dreamstime.com:
©Geraktv: pg. 10 (background), ©Avemar82: pg. 13, ©Rozi81: pg.
15, ©Mtsue pg. 33 (sign), endsheets ©Miragik

ISBN-13: 978-1939487-85-8
Library of Congress Control Number: 2017953571
First Printing, November 2017

Mutual Publishing, LLC
1215 Center Street, Suite 210
Honolulu, Hawaii 96816
Ph: (808) 732-1709
Fax: (808) 734-4094
e-mail: info@mutualpublishing.com
www.mutualpublishing.com

Printed in South Korea by Dong-A Printing

Introduction

Hawai'i fell in love with Rocky and Kaimana, Waikīkī's monk seals. Here was a good news story during an unending wave of bad news stories—from terrorist attacks, to contentious demonstrations, to international strife.

It was, and is, a story of both universal and local themes—a mother's love for her child, the mischievousness of youthful curiosity and growing independence, our duty to share the land, and the importance of protecting the environment and endangered species.

Not only was it a story for all ages and people everywhere (reported and shared across the mainland), it was easily accessible to witness because the backdrop was one of the busiest beaches in Hawai'i. The taking of photos and selfies was nonstop.

All who followed the story in print or visited Kaimana Beach in person witnessed Hawai'i at its best. We are presenting their story as a children's book that can be enjoyed and shared with people of all ages.

Melody Bentz Photography

Rocky is an endangered Hawaiian monk seal. She was born on the Island of Kauaʻi in the year 2000.

Rocky has had nine pups. This is good because Hawaiian monk seals are one of the most **ENDANGERED** marine mammals in the world.

Hawaiʻi only has two native mammals—the Hawaiian monk seal and the Hawaiian hoary bat.

KAUAʻI

Rocky on Kauaʻi • DB Dunlap

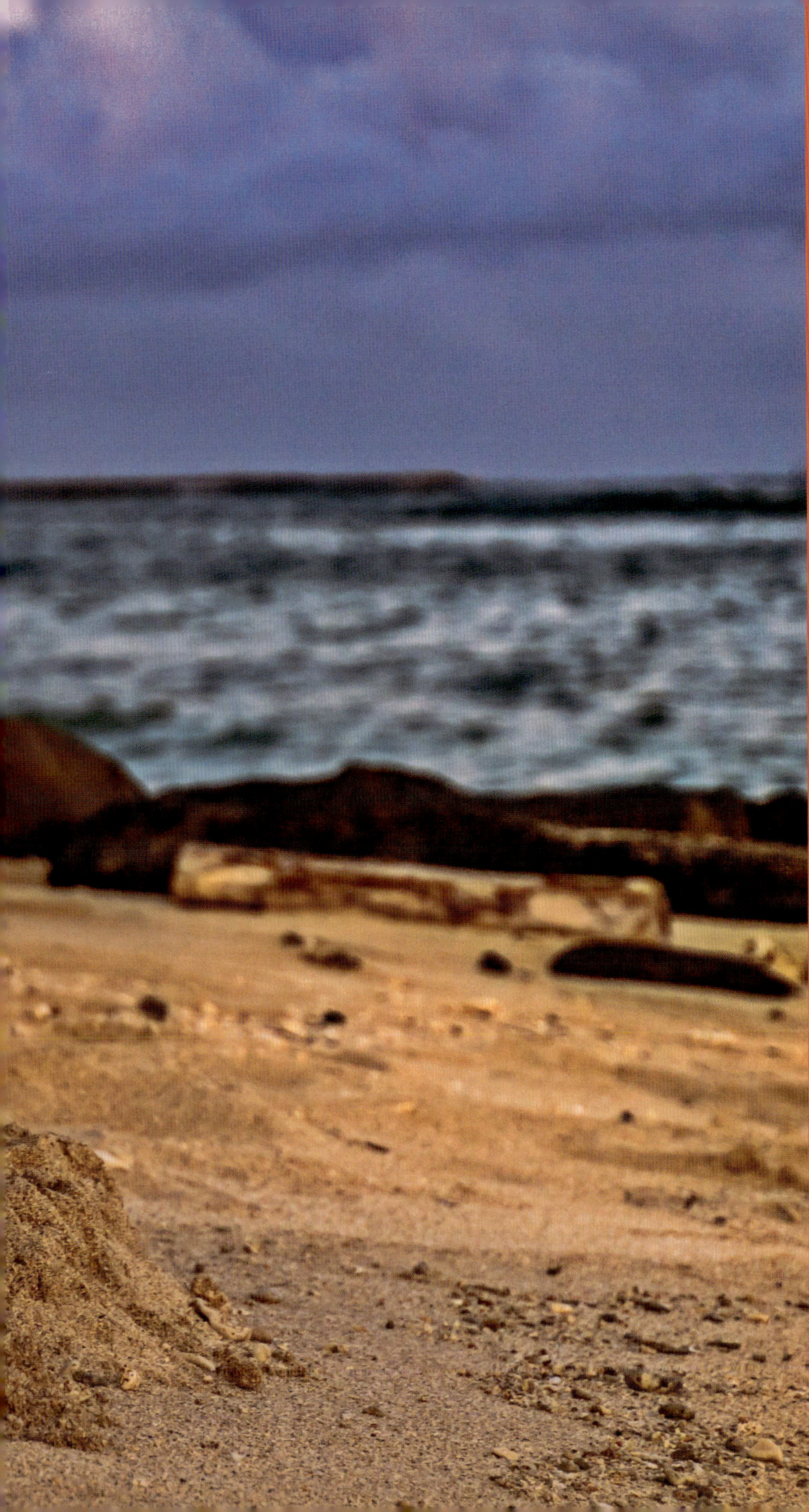

O'AHU

Rocky likes to visit the other islands, especially O'ahu where she spends much of her time.

Even though she likes to play along O'ahu's beaches, she always returns home to Kaua'i to give birth.

UNTIL ONE DAY...

wish you were here...

Douglas Peebles

Douglas Peebles

Kaimana Beach, Waikiki

Dennis Oda, *Honolulu Star-Advertiser*

Cindy Ellen Russell, *Honolulu Star-Advertiser*

Rocky decides to give birth to her tenth pup on the Island of Oʻahu on one of the busiest beaches in Waikīkī—

KAIMANA BEACH.

On a very early Thursday morning, Rocky gives birth to a healthy female pup.

Of course people nickname her

KAIMANA.

It's a Girl

Cindy Ellen Russell, *Honolulu Star-Advertiser*

HAWAIIAN MONK SEAL
MOM & PUP
NURSING & RESTING AREA

NO LOUD TALKING AROUND SEALS

AVOID EYE CONTACT WITH SEALS

NO LOUD CAMERA NOISES NEAR SEALS

Human disturbances may cause the mom to abandon her pup, condition the pup to being around people and/or create aggressive behavior.

Mother seals, like any wild animal, will defend their young. This man was bitten in the arm when he got between a mother monk seal and her pup.

Hawaiian monk seals are protected by both state and federal laws

Cindy Ellen Russell,
Honolulu Star-Advertiser

Officials from **NOAA*** rope off an area around Rocky and Kaimana to keep them safe from people and to give them space to nurse and rest.

* National Oceanic and Atmospheric Administration

FOOTNOTE
2

Cindy Ellen Russell, *Honolulu Star-Advertiser*

Rocky is a good mom. She is very protective of her newborn pup.

A **PLASTIC BAG** blowing in the wind passes too close to Kaimana. Rocky barks and chases it away.

FOOTNOTE

3

Many people come
to visit Rocky and
Kaimana.

It's a rare sight to see
a monk seal and her
newborn baby in busy
Waikīkī.

People take lots and
lots of pictures and
selfies.

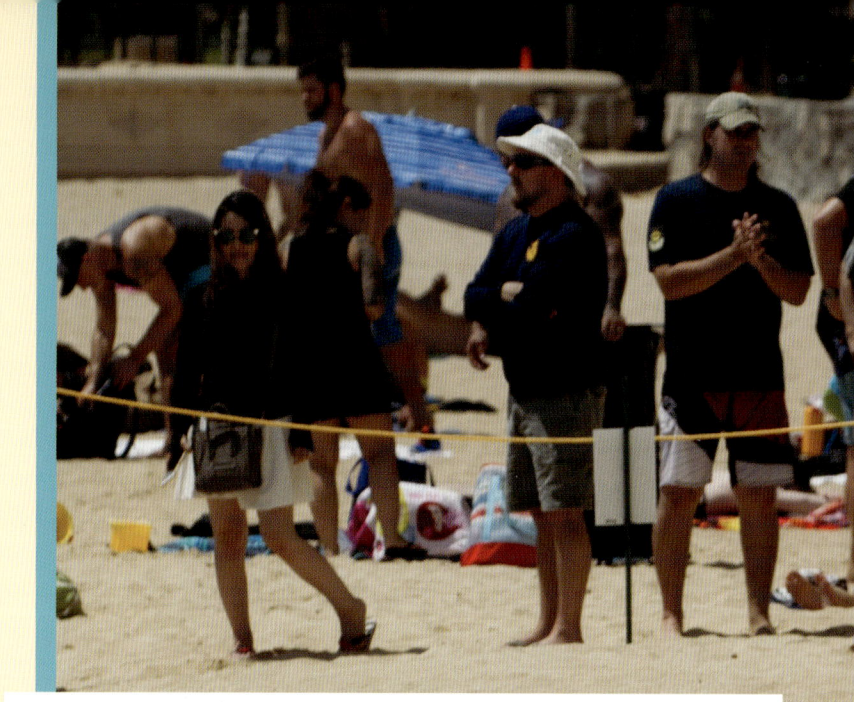

Kyle Harada

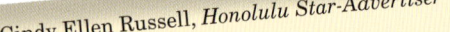

Cindy Ellen Russell, *Honolulu Star-Advertiser*

Shhhh...
I'm Sleeping

Cindy Ellen Russell, *Honolulu Star-Advertiser*

Cindy Ellen Russell, *Honolulu Star-Advertiser*

Rocky and Kaimana won't stay in Waikīkī for long.

They are expected to remain on the beach for about forty days. Kaimana needs time to grow strong enough to swim long distances.

Cindy Ellen Russell, *Honolulu Star-Advertiser*

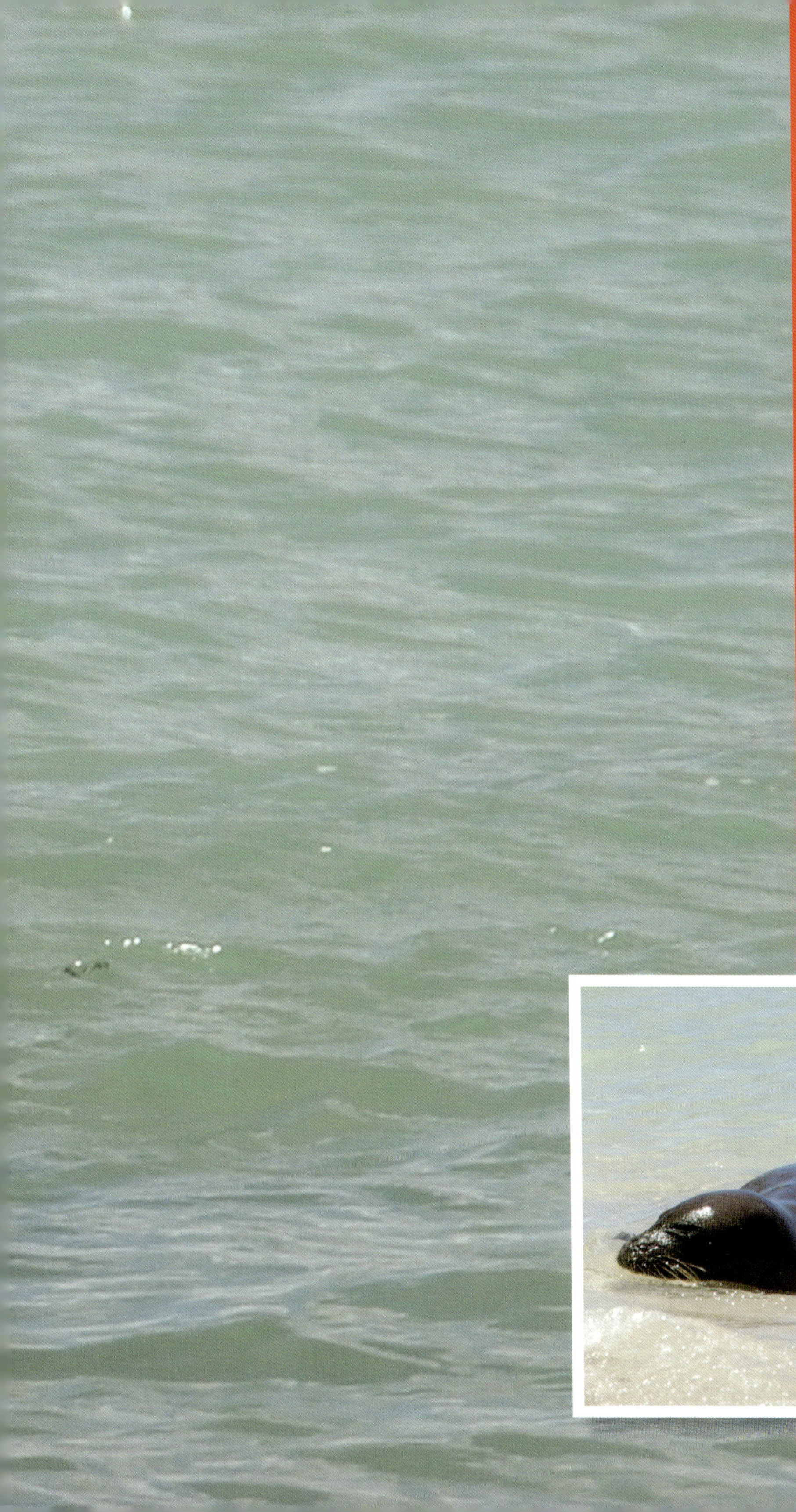

Kaimana is growing quickly. She swims with her mom in the waters off Waikīkī.

Officials warn swimmers to stay far away from them as they swim. Rocky is still a very protective mom.

Craig T. Kojima, *Honolulu Star-Advertiser*

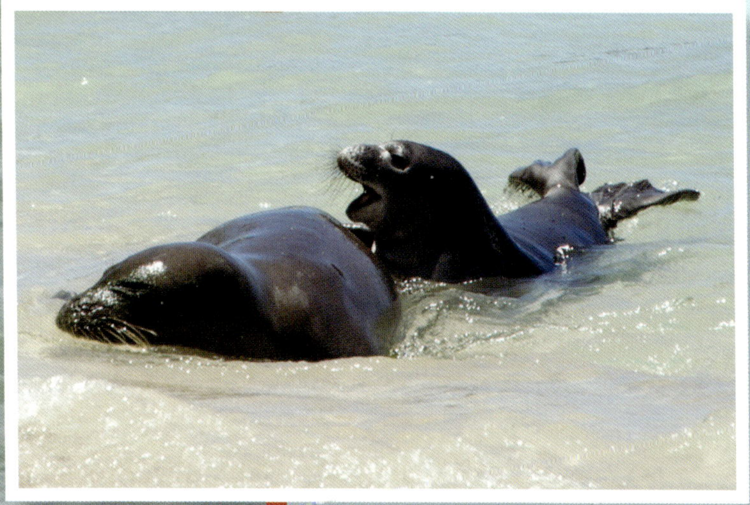

Marilyn Dunlap

Gayle Matsuda

When Kaimana is almost a month old, she and Rocky explore a nearby stretch of beach in front of the famous Outrigger Canoe Club. Kaiwi, another popular Hawaiian monk seal in Waikīkī, joins them to play. Officials "seal" off this new section of beach to keep everyone safe. But one day, Kaiwi gets too close to Kaimana while swimming and Rocky charges at her to protect little Kaimana.

Gayle Matsuda

Melody Bentz Photography

Kaimana is a curious little pup. She decides to go on an adventure without her mom. Kaimana goes for a swim in the nearby Natatorium.

ROCKY CAN'T FIND KAIMANA!

Worried, she calls out in distress.

Dennis Oda, Honolulu Star-Advertiser

Douglas Peebles

Dennis Oda, *Honolulu Star-Advertiser*

CAUTION

ENDANGERED
HAWAIIAN MONK SEAL

PLEASE DO NOT APPROACH

CALL: 1-808-220-7802

Seals need to rest on the beach and are protected by **Federal and State law**.

To report marine mammal emergencies and seal sightings, please call:
1-888-256-9840

MAHALO FOR YOUR KOKUA

Cindy Ellen Russell,
Honolulu Star-Advertiser

When Rocky finds Kaimana at the Natatorium, they swim together and rest on this new section of beach.

Officials rope off their new play area to keep them safe.

Dennis Oda, *Honolulu Star-Advertiser*

Dennis Oda, *Honolulu Star-Advertiser*

Bruce Asato,
Honolulu Star-Advertiser

Rocky and Kaimana
spend their days swimming,
visiting the Natatorium,
and rolling in the surf.
Life is good in Waikīkī.

Craig T. Kojima, *Honolulu Star-Advertiser*

Reverend Elias Parker performs a blessing ceremony for Rocky and Kaimana—a tradition in Hawai'i to mark beginnings like Kaimana's new journey in life.

Craig T. Kojima, *Honolulu Star-Advertiser*

Kaimana is growing bigger, stronger, and braver. She is becoming independent.

Once Kaimana is fully **WEANED**, Rocky will leave for the open ocean to feed.

It is time for Rocky to let Kaimana swim on her own.

At first, Kaimana is sad. But she soon starts to have fun on her own.

(both photos)
Bruce Asato, *Honolulu Star-Advertiser*

CAUTION
MONK SEAL
AT PLAY

Bruce Asato, *Honolulu Star-Advertiser*

Officials are worried about Kaimana. They don't want her to get too comfortable around so many people. Kaimana needs to be with other monk seals. She needs to learn how to hunt, and eat, and play like other monk seals.

One early morning, Kaimana is gently wrapped in a net and moved to a quiet, remote beach where she can play with other monk seals.

Jim Borg,
Honolulu Star-Advertiser

Jim Borg, *Honolulu Star-Advertiser*

Kaimana is happy in her new home. She wears a **TRACKING DEVICE** so NOAA can make sure she stays safe and happy.

Everyone who came to visit Kaimana in Waikīkī misses her, but they understand that she will be happier in a place with more monk seals and less people.

Hopefully both Rocky and Kaimana will visit Waikīkī beach again.

Melody Bentz Photography

See footnote 6 for an update!

Melody Bentz Photography

Star Advertiser

June 30, 2017

Monk seal Rocky gives birth in Waikiki, thrilling visitors

By Gary T. Kubota

Hawaiian monk seal RH58, also known as Rocky, gave birth to a healthy pup at Kaimana Beach in Waikiki late Wednesday or early Thursday. At top, people gathered behind the cordoned off area where the two seals are located.

June 30, 2017

HAWAI'I MAGAZINE.COM

"Rocky," an endangered Hawaiian monk seal, gives birth on Kaimana Beach in Waikiki

By Tracy Chan

HAWAII NEWS NOW

July 7, 2017

State: Keep your distance from nursing monk seal at Kaimana Beach

Star Advertiser

July 4, 2017

Monk seal mom and pup require wider berth over next few weeks

By Dan Nakaso

Rocky and her infant pup were on the shore Monday afternoon at Kaimana Beach in Waikiki. The National Oceanic and Atmospheric Administration's monk seal research program will be taking measures to ensure the well-being of the pair and the public's safety during today's Fourth of July holiday.

Star Advertiser

July 8, 2017

Officials reinforce warning to avoid mother monk seal

By Bianca Smallwood

Officials are reissuing warnings for the public to stay away from the Hawaiian monk seal named Rocky and her offspring on Kaimana Beach in Waikiki. The monk seal could become more aggressive as she nurses the pup, which is starting to move around.

Khon 2

July 18, 2017

Monk seal teaches pup to swim off Waikiki

Khon 2

July 19, 2017

Swimmers urged to stay out of ocean following

Star Advertiser

July 20, 2017

Video of protective seal mom cited in alert to beachgoers

By Bianca Smallwood

Star Advertiser

July 30, 2017

Pup is returned to mom after visit to Natatorium

By Leila Fujimori

Rocky and her pup were separated Friday night when Kaimana swam away and into the Waikiki Natatorium. The two were reunited on Kaimana Beach later that night when the pup was brought back to mom wrapped up in a borrowed beach blanket. The public is asked to keep its distance and avoid disturbing the pair, which experts think will be at the beach for another two weeks or so.

Hawaiʻi Public Radio

July 20, 2017

Hometown Waikiki: Hawaiian Monk Seal Mama and Her Pup

By Noe Tanigawa

August 4, 2017

Star Advertiser

Baby seal takes another dip, until mama shows up

By Leila Fujimori

Monk seal Rocky and her pup Kaimana drew a ⸻ day on Kaimana Beach in Waikiki after swimm⸻ rium pool.

Star Advertiser

August 5, 2017

There's someone swimming in the Natatorium

U.S.News & WORLD REPORT

July 30, 2017

Baby Monk Seal Reunited with Mother After Wandering Off

Khon 2

July 20, 2017

Wildlife officials ramp up warnings after close call with Waikiki swimmers, monk seals

August 9, 2017

Star Advertiser

Solo time nears for baby monk seal

By Timothy Hurley

Kaimana, the juvenile Hawaiian monk seal, swam alone in the waters off Kaimana Beach on Friday for nearly two hours. Her mother, Rocky, appeared to have disappeared after heading out to sea after nursing Kaimana, perhaps for the final time.

Star Advertiser

August 9, 2017

Baby monk seal will be relocated after weaning

By Timothy Hurley

Baby Hawaiian monk seal Kaimana and her mother, Rocky⸻ Tuesday in Waikiki as the Rev. Elias Parker gathered seawa⸻ seals. Experts have made the decision to move Kaimana af⸻ area where she is less likely to have human interaction and ⸻ hazards such as the Waikiki Natatorium.

August 13, 2017

Star Advertiser

A runaway seal reminds people of our inseparable kinship

By Mindy Pennybacker

Hawaiian monk seal mom Rocky and pup Kaimana played Tuesday in the waters off Kaimana Beach.

Khon 2

August 11, 2017

Next phase begins for young monk seal at Kaimana Beach

August 13, 2017

Star Advertiser

Seal pup moved to new home in the wild

By Jim Borg

Dennis Oda,
Honolulu Star-Advertiser

The Hawaiian Monk Seal

Craig T. Kojima, *Honolulu Star-Advertiser*

Hawaiian monk seals live between twenty-five and thirty years, on average.

They grow to about seven to seven-and-a-half feet in length, and an adult can weigh 375 to 450 pounds. Sometimes though, they grow longer—to eight feet—and even heavier—up to 600 pounds!

Their diet is mainly fish, cephalopods like squids and octopi, and crustaceans, like crabs and lobsters.

Hawaiian monk seal females mature at five to six years of age and can begin pupping, or having babies. Monk seal pups gestate, or grow in their mothers' tummies, for ten to eleven months.

Most pups are born in late March and early April, though year-round pup births have been recorded.

People who saw Kaimana right after she was born at the end of June, 2017, say she was like a little black furry bag, about two feet, or maybe two-and-a-half feet long. They guess that she weighed maybe twenty pounds—as much as a large bag of rice from the grocery store.

At the time she was born, Kaimana was so little and skinny officials could not tell if she was a boy or a girl. Even monk seal experts can't tell if a pup is a girl or a boy until it grows and gains weight. Then, when a pup rolls on its back to bask in the sun, people can see its belly, and know if it is male or female.

Newborn pups are black, and they molt, or shed their coat, when they are weaned.

By the Fourth of July, little Kaimana had grown a lot and weighed about forty pounds. Officials could only guess, based on their expert knowledge of seals, because nobody was allowed to get close enough to put Kaimana on a scale.

When volunteers picked up Kaimana from the beach to move her to her new home, she weighed between 180 and 200 pounds, and was about forty inches around.

The Hawaiian Monk Seal is Endangered

Hawaiian monk seals are often described as "critically endangered," but what does that mean?

The Hawaiian monk seal is the last remaining tropical seal species left in the world and only lives in waters around the Hawaiian Islands and remote, uninhabited parts of the islands.

Some scientists say they are one of the most endangered marine mammal species in the world.

The number of monk seals in the ocean was dropping for many years, but in 2013, the population started growing a little bit each year. Between 2013 and 2017, the population grew to 1,400 from 1,100.

Around the main Hawaiian Islands there are about 300 monk seals with roughly forty to fifty on the Island of Oʻahu as well as a small offshore islet called Rabbit Island. The rest of the population lives mostly around islands without cities and few people living on them.

To protect Hawaiian monk seals, laws in the state of Hawaiʻi are more strict than federal laws.

Because they are so rare, harming a monk seal can result in a fine of up to $50,000 and up to five years in jail.

Hawaiian monk seals spend most of their time in the ocean where they hunt for fish, sea creatures like squids and octopi, and shellfish.

When seals come ashore to lie in the sun or to give birth to their pups, officials tell people to stay at least fifty feet away from them. That's about the length of three minivans parked in a row lengthwise.

When a seal pup starts venturing into the water, with or without its mother, officials want people to stay at least 100 feet, or six minivan-lengths away. A mother seal is very protective of its pup. She doesn't want anyone, even another seal, to go near her baby.

Giving the seals so much space allows the seals to feel safe and also gives people a safe place to watch these rare and interesting marine mammals.

Cindy Ellen Russell, *Honolulu Star-Advertiser*

Kaimana Beach

Kaimana Beach is very popular with Hawai'i residents, and there are usually more local people than visitors there.

Because Rocky's seal pup was born at Kaimana Beach, people decided to nickname her Kaimana before anybody could tell if she was a girl or a boy seal.

When Kaimana was born thousands of people, both locals and visitors from around the world, came to the beach to see the mother and baby seal and take pictures and video of them.

The two seals became Internet sensations!

The place where Rocky decided to give birth to her now very famous pup used to be a very rocky bit of shoreline. After the Waikīkī Natatorium was built there, ocean currents created a wide sandy beach in the spot.

Some people call it Sans Souci Beach, after a hotel that used to be there way back in 1893. Sans Souci is a French term that means "without worries."

Kaz Tanabe

Some people took to calling the beach "Kaimana," which is a way to pronounce the word "diamond" in Hawaiian. The beach is near Diamond Head crater, one of the most famous landmarks in Hawai'i.

The hotel that now stands on the site is called the New Otani Kaimana Beach Hotel.

Kaz Tanabe

The Waikīkī Natatorium

The Waikīkī Natatorium War Memorial was opened in 1927 as a living memorial to thousands of men and women from Hawai'i who served in World War I.

It is a salt water pool built in the ocean on Waikīkī's Sans Souci Beach, also known as Kaimana Beach. It is very old and has been closed to the public since the 1980s, but a group of people is working to raise the money needed to restore the pool, as well as the stands where people would sit to watch famous Olympic swimmers.

Olympic gold-medalist and famous Hawai'i waterman, Duke Kahanamoku, was the first to swim in the pool which opened on his birthday. Other famous swimmers from Hawai'i who swam at the Natatorium were Johnny Weissmuller and Buster Crabbe. They went on to become famous Hollywood movie stars.

Many generations of people in Hawai'i grew up swimming in the Natatorium, both in races and for fun, and are sad that it is closed.

Because it is old and dangerous to walk around and swim in, the Natatorium was closed to the public many years ago. When baby Kaimana decided to enter the Natatorium from the ocean side, people were worried that Kaimana might get hurt or trapped. Officials had to very carefully guide in the volunteers who walked in to rescue her, so they would not be hurt.

The people successfully carried Kaimana out of the Natatorium with a blanket and put her back on the beach where she could easily find her mother.

Hawai'i State Archives

Douglas Peebles

Hawaiian Monk Seals and People

As cute and cuddly looking as baby Hawaiian monk seals are, with their big eyes and playful personalities, they are wild animals and are not meant to be pets.

Their playful personalities led Hawaiians, centuries ago, to call them "ilio holo i ka uaua" which means "dog that runs in rough water."

But monk seals are not like a family dog that likes to play with people.

Sometimes, if people get too close to Hawaiian monk seals—especially if they get close to mothers with pups—the mother may charge and attack to keep their new pups safe.

Baby Kaimana was born on one of the busiest beaches in all of Hawai'i, which is unusual. Hawaiian monk seals normally choose beaches with no people on them in order to have their pups.

Because there were so many people around Rocky and Kaimana all the time, officials and volunteers worked hard to

Dennis Oda, *Honolulu Star-Advertiser*

protect them from people by putting up a fence to keep people a safe distance away.

It is not good for Hawaiian monk seals to have too much contact with humans, because seals and humans live in different worlds.

Experts don't want people to feed the seals, because people and seals eat different foods and people food would not be healthy for the seals.

It might seem like it would be fun to play with a baby Hawaiian monk seal, but experts say that could make the seals act differently than they would if they were just playing with other monk seals, like they do in the ocean.

Once Rocky decided Kaimana was ready to take care of herself, officials knew it would be better for Kaimana to move to a secret location. That way, she could hunt for food and find other Hawaiian monk seals to play with.

Cindy Ellen Russell, *Honolulu Star-Advertiser*

The Waikīkī Aquarium

Even though Kaimana was moved to a new home, you can meet the endangered Hawaiian monk seals that live at the Waikīkī Aquarium. It is only a five-minute walk from the beach where Kaimana was born and spent the first part of her life.

The two monk seals at the Waikīkī Aquarium are males and their names are Maka onaona and Hoʻailona.

The seals were rescued when they were pups, and since they would not have been able to survive in the wild, they were given a home at the Waikīkī Aquarium. There, visitors love to see them basking in the sun and swimming around in their pool.

There are many, many exhibits at the Waikīkī Aquarium where you can see bright, colorful fish, and more marvels of the ocean, like unusual sea creatures that you would not be able to see if you were just swimming at the beach.

The Waikīkī Aquarium wants people to appreciate Pacific marine life and is active in working with the University of

Waikīkī Aquarium

Hawaiʻi and marine conservation officials to help protect endangered species like the Hawaiian monk seal and Hawaiian green sea turtle, or honu.

The aquarium is open almost every day of the year from 9 a.m. to 4:30 p.m., though it has shorter hours on Thanksgiving Day and New Year's Day. It is closed only on Christmas Day and the one day of the year that the Honolulu Marathon is run. But don't worry, while it may not be open to the public, aquarium employees still make sure all the animals are fed.

The aquarium offers a kamaʻāina rate so Hawaiʻi's families can enjoy all the exhibits at a discounted price.

https://www.waikikiaquarium.org/

Waikīkī Aquarium

Learn More About Hawaiian Monk Seals

Visit these websites:

- Department of Land and Natural Resources (DLNR)
  Safe viewing guidelines for viewing endangered Hawaiian monk seals, a video by the state of Hawaii Department of Natural Resources:
  https://vimeo.com/225164605

- National Oceanic and Atmospheric Administration (NOAA)
  Fisheries Division—Hawaiian Monk Seal
  http://www.fisheries.noaa.gov/pr/species/mammals/seals/hawaiian-monk-seal.html

- Protected species— Hawaiian Monk Seal
  http://www.fpir.noaa.gov/PRD/prd_hms_index.html

- Pacific Island Region Marine Mammal Response Network:
  http://www.fpir.noaa.gov/PRD/prd_marine_mammal_response.html

- Hawai'i Marine Animal Response
  http://h-mar.org/

- Kaua'i-based monk seal observers:
  https://kauaiseals.wordpress.com/

- Marine Mammal Center—Ke Kai Ola
  http://www.marinemammalcenter.org/what-we-do/ke-kai-ola/

- The Nature Conservancy—Hawaiian monk seals
  https://is.gd/NC_MonkSeals

**If you encounter a stranded or entangled marine mammal, please call:
Marine Mammal Stranding and Entanglement Hotline
1- 888-256-9840 (toll free)**

Acknowledgments

Mahalo to the Honolulu *Star-Advertiser* photographers, the news bloggers, and the fans of Hawaiian monk seals who have followed Rocky and documented her life in the Islands. A special thanks to Donna Festa, Gayle Matsuda, DB Dunlap (aka the monk seal whisperer who named Rocky) and Marilyn Dunlap of the blog Monksealmania.blogspot.com, Kyle Harada of Jeffsetters.com, and Melody Bentz of MelodyBentzPhotography.com for their beautiful photographs of Rocky and Kaimana. Their love for Rocky, Kaimana, and all the Hawaiian monk seals in the Islands shows through their work and dedication in documenting and preserving the lives of these amazing creatures.

Footnotes

If an animal is endangered, it means that it is at serious risk of becoming extinct and that animal will no longer exist on Earth. Animals become extinct for a number of reasons. Sometimes it is because they are over-hunted. Sometimes it is due to disease. The once-thriving Caribbean monk seal, a sort of cousin to the Hawaiian monk seal that lived in the Caribbean Sea and Gulf of Mexico, (alternately, the Atlantic Ocean), is now extinct. There are no more because they were hunted by humans. It is important to keep Hawaiian monk seals on Earth, so laws have been put in place to keep them from becoming extinct. By designating them as endangered, people know not to harm them.

The Office of Protected Resources in NOAA's National Marine Fisheries Service is part of the U.S. government. It is responsible for protecting marine mammals like Rocky and Kaimana, and whales and dolphins, but also for protecting endangered and threatened marine life of all types.

Plastic things, like bags, water bottles, and fishing nets, are dangerous for marine animals. They accidentally eat plastic or can get tangled up in it causing injury.

Monk seal pups like Kaimana grow strong by drinking their mother's milk. When Kaimana no longer needs her mother's milk and is ready to eat fish and other food from the ocean, Rocky won't have to stay on the beach with Kaimana any longer. She will leave Kaimana to hunt for food on her own.

Kaimana now wears a tracking device, given to her by NOAA, so they can keep track of her whereabouts to make sure she stays safe and to study her movements. The device will likely fall off during her first molting at one year of age. The device will not bother her at all.

UPDATE! On Labor Day, Sept. 4, 2017, Kaimana was spotted with a hook and lure hanging from her mouth by volunteers from Hawai'i Marine Animal Response. Luckily, she was able to shake it free resulting in a small wound, but no infection. NOAA and DLNR reminds fishermen to take care when casting and to collect all their gear after leaving a fishing sitc.

Kalākaua Ave

Outrigger
Canoe Club

New Otani
Kaimana Beach
Hotel

Kaimana
Beach

War Memorial
Natatorium

Waikīkī
Aquarium

Melody Bentz Photography

48